No Money

Down

Defying the myth that it takes money to

make money

GENE SWANK

Contents

Foreword

Gene is the best person I know to teach founders how to build a successful business from scratch. He has done it himself many times. What impresses me most is that he didn't start with a large bank account, a vast network of contacts or unlimited resources. Instead, he had an idea and $100 in his pocket and he turned that into a global, multi-million dollar e-commerce business through hard work, creativity, persistence and sheer determination. He has experienced, many times over, the highs and lows that are involved in being an entrepreneur and launching a startup. Gene is a sincere and passionate founder, mentor, investor and board member who has helped many people achieve a level of success they didn't believe was possible. I've seen it firsthand.

In *No Money Down*, Gene shares his valuable experiences, insights and lessons learned. He shows you how to get started, the keys to success, what to expect along the way and how to deal with the bumps in the road. He provides a clear and concise blueprint for how to proceed. This book is a must read for anyone looking to start a business and a valuable resource you'll come back to again and again.

David Dowling

Chief Marketing Officer, Communications Segment, United Online

Introduction

So you wanna be a business owner? You've talked about it. All your friends know your business idea, but you still haven't taken action. What's holding you back? What are you afraid of? Why don't you just start? Well, today is your day. Today is the day that we, together, are going to take the leap. No more are you going to simply talk, talk, talk about your business. Today we are going to start the process. It may be as simple as finding out if that business that you've been talking about for years, even has legs. Can it actually even work as a business? More than anything else, we are going to discover, together, in this book, how to get the mentality that is required to start and grow your business. We're going to move away for that old saying that it takes money to make money and realize that, regardless of your financial situation, a thriving venture is within your reach. Now, this doesn't mean that you need to quit your job tomorrow because you're going to be rich the day after. It just means that you need to take a good hard look at where you are right now and start the process towards reaching your goals.

Chapter 1 Genesis

The life that I live today, sometimes even to myself feels like a dream. I've been blessed with amazing children, a gorgeous wife and a career that I truly love. The coolest thing about this dream is that it's real. More than anything else, what taking the leap in my own life and becoming a business owner has done for me, is that it's bought me time. I used to spend my time driving back and forth, sometimes as much as 3 to 4 hours per day commuting to and from work. I would leave for work before the sun would rise and before the rest of my family had even woke up. To make things even worse, most days I would get home after the sun had already set for the day. I was rarely able to attend to my kids sporting events & going to their performances at school was always a challenge. Some weeks it felt like I never even saw them at all. Now we have that house... I remember when my wife and I first got married, she said that she didn't even care if we lived in a trailer as long as we owned our own place. Well, now we own nine properties. Now I can spend that time with my family. One of our properties is on the beach. And yes, I definitely use it as an income source, but when I wanna spend a week on the beach, I have my own place that I can go to. I'm my own boss. It's allowed me to have the marriage, the family and the relationships that I've always wanted. More importantly, it affords me the opportunity to give back and help others nearly every single day.

I'm so delighted to be able to share this with you because the truth is that even though today I run several successful companies, own a fair amount of real estate, and manage a startup incubator that has a combined portfolio worth over $150M, life was not always this way. There was a time in my life when I could barely afford to pay for the room that I was renting or even food to put in my stomach.

I want to share with you a little about my early years because, let's be honest, if I can make it happen, so can you. Around the age of eight, my health began to decline. I spent the majority of the next few years in and out of doctor's offices and hospital beds. Amongst my ailments was severe asthma that was triggered by my allergies to almost everything. So I spent a lot of time indoors and alone. I remember when my health was at its worst, the doctors told my mother that I would eventually recover, but joked that I would never be a star athlete.

By the time I was a freshman in high school, my asthma seemed to be under control and my new doctor suggested that I start playing sports to build up my lung capacity. Well, I was the kid that could barely walk up a flight of stair without bursting into a coughing fit, how was I going to play sports. I remember thinking that everyone was going to laugh at me. They did indeed, but instead of letting that bother me, I just decided that I was going to push myself harder than anyone else and that would make all the difference. The first sport that I tried was Football. I had never even watched Football before, but that didn't stop me from giving it my all. I was a quick study and got to play on the Freshman team that year. In the winter, I joined the wrestling team and then track & field. I remember listening to the motivational pregame speeches that the coaches would deliver. I'd never heard anything like that before, this resonated with me and made me want to work even harder. I remember coming home from practice, exhausted every single day, but would continue to train. I'd run up & down the stairs in my house, go to the weight room at school every morning and push myself as hard as I possibly could. The competition may have been bigger, faster and more experienced, but I would outwork them. I had something to prove and wanted it more than they did. During my freshman track season, I was chosen as a distance runner, which seems like a strange choice for a kid with respiratory issues. After a lot of hard work, I eventually started winning a few races, and even the kids from the rival schools started to recognize me as a contender. I racked up several medals that year and was one of only a few kids that year to receive a varsity letter as a freshman.

In the next few years, I went on to go to be a starter on the Football team, go to the state championship twice in Track and become an all-state nominee in wrestling. So in other words, the kid that was told he would never be a star athlete did, in fact, do quite well. Why was I able to achieve this? The doctors said it wasn't possible. Perhaps it was because I simply didn't know any better. I'd forgotten about the doctor's predictions because I was too focused on reaching my goals.

Did you know, that for decades there was a common consensus that the human body was not physically capable of running a mile in under 4 minutes? This was a barrier that was beyond the physical limitations of our bodies... right? Well, on May 6th, 1954, Roger Bannister broke the 4-minute mile barrier with a time of 3 minutes, fifty-nine and four-tenths of a second. This may seem inconsequential, I mean he only broke the barrier by a fraction of a second, right? Maybe there was an issue with the equipment? I mean this isn't physically possible, right? The strange thing is, that within the next year more and more athletes began to run sub-four-minute miles and the current count of athletes that have broken this barrier is in the thousands. How can we explain this phenomenon? Did our bodies evolve overnight? The reality is that nothing changed with our physical abilities, the bar was simply moved and our mindset changed.

Throughout your entrepreneurial journey, you will likely be told that your goals are unreasonable and sometimes even irrational. Don't let dogma hold you back from doing something that you know you are capable of doing. Just because society tells you it is impossible doesn't mean you should give up on your dreams. Just like Roger Bannister broke the 4-minute mile barrier and moved the bar of what we now believe our bodies are physically capable of doing, so can you.

Back to the story... So let's skip forward a few years to college. While in college, the internet was just starting to pick up some momentum, and then we went through what was known as the "dot com" boom. During this time, you could literally slap a dot com on virtually anything and someone would probably give you a million dollars to go out and make it. Well, those days didn't last very long. Just like the housing bubble in 2008, this bubble eventually popped. Unfortunately for me, I happened to graduate from college right after this collapse and with a technology-focused degree. I know technology experts that were forced to go from $100k per year salaries to pizza delivery jobs because that is the only work they could find. Unfortunately, I made a few bad decisions during this time in my life and within the next couple of years, I found myself flat broke. When I say I was broke, I mean seriously broke, like my cell phone was shut off and my bank account was not just zero, it was negative.

I found a job working for a factory making just above minimum wage. I remember driving across town and taking my paychecks to the issuing bank to cash them because I knew that if I deposited it into my bank account, it would go towards that negative balance. Well, one day I decided that I wanted to change my life, so I began saving up some cash and using the computers at the library to apply for jobs in my spare time. I was excited when I heard back from a company in San Diego. We set up a phone interview, and it couldn't have gone better. They wanted me to come in for an "in person" interview. It was mostly a formality they told me, but travel expenses from my current residence in Missouri to California were my responsibility. I quickly realized that I didn't have enough cash saved up to make the trip to California and back, so I had to make a tough decision. I was so passionate about improving my situation, so I packed up everything that I owned into my car and took off across the country. I had saved just enough money to make it to San Diego, pay for my first month of rent and have a little bit of flexibility in case I ran into any unexpected expenses or in case my first check took some time to get issued. I can not express in words, the immense excitement that I was experiencing as I made the cross country voyage.

For those of you that aren't familiar with Missouri, it is relatively flat, there are a few large rolling hills, but definitely, nothing that resembles a California mountain by any means. During my cross country voyage, I was concerned about saving money on gas but remembered reading somewhere that using cruise control might improve the mpg. So while going through an especially large and mountainous area in the middle of the desert, I pressed the cruise control button and began to day-dream about my new life in California. Little would I know that something as small as pressing a button in the middle of the desert would permanently alter the trajectory of my life forever.

While driving up the mountainside (with cruise control on), my car suddenly began to smoke and then the gas pedal went all the way to the floor. The engine began to roar. I guided the car off the road and quickly realized that my transmission had burnt up. I still to this day, am not 100% sure if I was told the honest truth, but the only repairman in that small desert town in which I was now stranded, informed me that my transmission had burnt out because I was using cruise control while going up a mountainside. He explained that you're not supposed to use overdrive while going up a steep mountain and that this mistake is what caused my transmission to give. If you've never had a transmission replaced, then you may not know how incredibly expensive they can be (especially when there is only one repair shop in town, and they don't care about your sob story of being broke). I had no choice, but to pay for the repair. By the time I arrived in San Diego and paid for my first month of rent, I had $20 cash left in my pocket, no credit cards, no phone, very little gas in the car, a few snacks to munch on and a negative bank balance. At first, I panicked, but then I realized that I would be getting this awesome job soon, so no need to worry. Well, you may remember that my phone had been shut off and getting a transmission fixed in the middle of the desert can take a few days. This delay had caused me to miss the interview, with no way to let them know that I would be late, but I had no need to worry because they loved me and thought I was a perfect fit. When I finally checked in with the company, they informed me that they had given the position to someone else, because they hadn't heard from me and thought I was unreliable. I remember that moment very clearly. I remember the feeling of intense hopelessness, it felt like someone had punched me directly in the gut. I was in a new town with no job, no prospects, no money, and $20 to my name. I remember feeling physically ill and dropping to my knees. I looked up to the sky and wanted to shout at the top of my lungs, but instead said internally to myself, "Why God, is this happening to me." The feelings of hopelessness were overwhelming, I had done everything correctly, how could this one small mistake derail all of my goals of having a better life. I had made this voyage and sacrificed every penny of my savings because I was going to change my life, but now the future looked so very bleak. I realized that my stomach was empty and soon another months rent would be due, so I gave myself 24 hours to be depressed and dwell on all my problems and then decided once again, it is time to pull myself up by the bootstraps and get busy finding a job. I knew that being depressed would not solve my problems, I was hungry, literally, and figuratively.

I ended up going to a temporary job agency and telling them that I would do any job that they had. I didn't care if I had to scrub toilets or answer phones, I was going to turn my life around. That would require money. The agency told me that they had a position that actually matched my "skill set" and it was at a technology company, but it was basically pushing buttons and writing down results from tests, oh and it only paid $12 an hour. I was so excited to have the opportunity that I immediately accepted and got started working right away. I remember my first day of work and meeting my new boss, Jeff Rivard. Jeff was a brilliant RF engineer. We immediately hit it off. I realized that the manual calculations that we were doing could be easily automated, so I pitched an idea to automate the system to Jeff. I quickly realized that for the first time in my life, I had a boss that actually believed in me. He ran the idea all the way up to the top, but we were told that the company couldn't pay for me to build this type of solution, there just wasn't a budget for it. They jokingly told us that I could build it in my spare time. Well, I thought to myself... game on. I went home the next few nights and worked on the software that would help to automate these processes. When I presented the solution, it was a huge success and eventually led to my temporary contract getting converted into full-time employment. The original contract with this company was for a week but little did I know that I would spend the next 14 years, rising up the ranks and building my professional career at this organization.

During the first year with the company, they held a Christmas party, and everyone was allowed to bring a date. I didn't know anyone to invite, but luckily I had made a friend in the warehouse. He mentioned that his girlfriend knew someone that I should definitely meet. I still remember the moment when I first saw Tiara, she walked into the room, and my heart dropped to the floor. She was the most beautiful woman I had ever met, and I knew at that moment that someday she would be my wife. Tiara and I eventually got married, started a family, and built a beautiful life together. The truth is that I never realized that all of this was linked together until one day, my youngest son said something very strange to me. Out of the blue, he said: "dad, I'm so glad your car broke down," I couldn't possibly understand what he was talking about, so I informed him that it isn't very nice to be happy about someone's misfortunes. He then went on to remind me that I had told him the story of my car breaking down in the desert on the way to California. I still couldn't understand why this could make him happy, but then he continued to explain, he said, "dad, because, if your car didn't break down, I wouldn't be here today." All of a sudden in my head, the dots began to connect. I realized that everything truly amazing that I hold so dear in my life was born from an event that was so incredibly painful and full of despair. The truth is, that something as small as pressing the wrong button in my car while driving through the desert would change my life forever and put me on the path that I was meant to be traveling. I tell you this story because in the moment, sometimes things don't make sense and you can't understand why something so painful has happened to you, but the truth is, these events are the necessary catalysts that make us into the person that we were designed to be. It doesn't make sense in the moment, but I challenge you to connect the dots, and I would dare to guess that some of the most amazing events in your life can be traced back to an event that seemed so awful that it rocked you to the core. As you build your business and begin the sometimes long road to reaching your dreams, you will likely incur a lot of very painful roadblocks. It is necessary to remind yourself that these challenges are simply part of the process, stay focused, and continue to work towards those goals.

Chapter 2 All I Need Is

Money

Most experts will tell you that a business fails because of a lack of money, well I believe that the real problem, in most instances, is a lack of passion and drive. It takes hustle and grit to build a business and a strong stomach that can weather a metaphorical punch in the gut. You must be lean and flexible, with the ability to shake off those failures and continue to persevere. Most companies shut down not because they are inherently failures, but because their founders gave up after the first few setbacks. The ultimate success of a business is based only about 10% on how great the actual "idea" is. The other 90% is based on how well that idea is executed. It is very common for even seasoned entrepreneurs to make a ton of mistakes and fail the first time around, but a hiccup or two does not mean the business is unviable. Learn from those mistakes, listen to the market, and have the confidence that you will eventually reach your business goals.

I love to tell stories because I think they help things hit home. I want to tell you a story about two friends. These friends worked together, they lived together and would commute together down the always congested interstate 15 freeway every day. Well sometimes when traffic was looking a little nasty, they would take a shortcut down Del Dios road which goes through the heart of Rancho Santa Fe California. For those of you that are not familiar with San Diego geography, Rancho Santa Fe is a pretty upscale place to live. In fact, it's one of the most expensive places to live in the country. So, in other words, there are lots of big homes and fancy cars. One day traffic was especially bad. The friends decided to take their special shortcut. That day, the first friend said to the second, "I hate going this way... I absolutely despise it". The second friend, confused, asked for clarification, he couldn't understand why his travel buddy would want to sit in traffic. The first friend continued: "I hate going this way because I can't stand seeing all these huge mansions and exotic cars, because I know that that will never be me." Well the second friend, thought for a moment and then responded with "Well... I love going this way, I absolutely love it, because I love looking at all those big homes and fancy cars, because I know someday that's going to be me". Two friends that had similar experiences, but very different attitudes about their situations. Spoiler alert... One of those friends was actually me. Can you guess which one? I loved to take that route and to fantasize about someday reaping the rewards of my hard work. I could picture myself in a life that afforded me these luxuries, and it inspired me. The truth is that only one of us went on to build successful companies and make the sorta financial gains that would support the ability to live in that neighborhood (even though I eventually changed my mind about wanting to live there). My friend did go on to be relatively successful in his career and does make a decent living, but I honestly believe that the difference in attitude is why my ventures were successful. He later attempted to start a company of his own, which unfortunately came to a quick and unpleasant end.

Chapter 3 Raising Money Is Expensive

I've been extremely fortunate to have had the opportunity to mentor hundreds, if not thousands of startups. I must admit that one of the most common misconceptions that I've noticed most early stage (and sometimes even later stage) founders have, is that money is a magic cure that will solve all their problems. I can't even fathom how many times I've heard an entrepreneur claim: "If I only had another $200k..." when in reality, an investment is the last thing they actually need. Bringing in capital may be a necessity for your startup, but attempting to raise too early can lead to a whole slew of problem.

Raising money is expensive, I know this may sound crazy, but it can be a full-time job. Raising money can be very distracting, and if you're focused on the fundraising instead of just putting your head down and concentrating on building the business, it can sometimes do more harm than good. Most investors want to see traction before opening their wallets and let's be honest, the only person that really wants to invest in your unproven dreams, is probably your mother.

There are so many ways to prove your business model and tricks that you can use to reach those necessary KPIs, without spending your life savings. Let's assume that you find an investor that is interested in taking a chance on your company while it's still in the idea stage. The terms will likely be very onerous because you don't really have a way to prove your valuation, and the company has yet to be validated. If you haven't identified your target market yet, you may accidentally blow through your entire budget without having anything to show for it. This will, unfortunately, leave you in an awkward situation when you need to raise more capital. Investors will be more apprehensive about investing in your venture because your track record will show a tendency to blow through savings and not delivering the desired ROI. Have you ever heard the old adage that "it takes money to make money," well, I'd like to argue that this is not always the case. I will attempt to share with you throughout this book, several of the tips that I have used in the past to literally start a business with very little to no money.

Chapter 4 Building A Team

As the founder, it is imperative that you understand that the success of the company is greatly upon your shoulders. Often times others are going to let you down, so you have to be the glue that holds the organization together, even when those around you may lose sight and no longer share in the vision. Keeping that in mind, having an incredible team can make all the difference, so selecting team members that are a great cultural fit may be almost as important as their skill set.

Hiring a team can be expensive, even if you're paying them in sweat equity. Equity may seem worthless at the moment, but every time you issue shares, your slice of the pie gets a bit slimmer. Even 5% of a $100M dollar exit (likely much less after dilution), is a pretty big windfall for that early employee. Keep that in mind when negotiating their equity stake. They are being paid a salary, but it consists of stock that will someday (if everything goes according to plan) be magnitudes more valuable than the market rate salary.

If your company is building technology but your not a technical founder, you may want to consider bringing someone on as a technical co-founder. It's not always a necessity to make them a co-founder, but if the core of the business is centered around technology, you may want someone with a little more skin in the game to be in the trenches with you. Make sure you vet their technical aptitude (even if you need to utilize a third party resource to do so) and make sure they are a good cultural fit. Hiring is resource intensive, so do your best to ensure they share your overall vision and that you won't butt heads.

You may be asking yourself, how is it possible to convince someone to work for you, for equity only? How are they going to pay their bills? I know others may disagree with this, but I believe that it is perfectly acceptable for an employee to continue working their full-time job until the organization becomes stable enough to pay them out of profits or capital acquired through a fundraising event. Your potential team member may have a family to support and can't make the sacrifice of quitting their job for an unpaid gig, no matter how much they believe in the company. I prefer to have them work after hours if needed.

It may take a little longer, but it makes the likelihood of them being able to weather the storms with you, much higher.

Convincing the candidate to come on board in exchange for equity can be a bit tricky. I like to pitch the potential candidate in the same way you would pitch a potential investor. Make sure you tell a story that shows them the path to profitability. Get them excited about the company's mission and the impact it will make on the world. If you couldn't convince any potential partners to work for you on an equity basis, how would you be able to convince an investor to take a chance on you? It is a very similar conversation, in my opinion. In both instances, you have to convince them that their contribution (which is time vs money) will have an excellent ROI.

If you've not already set up an employee pool, I suggest speaking to your accountant and/or lawyer about doing so. I prefer to set aside at least 10% for future hires. This means the equity is already accounted for and allows you to hire others without diluting yourself or other co-founders. Also make sure you place the new hires on a vesting schedule, doing so prevents them from leaving in a week or so with a large ownership of the company.

Lastly, your new employee needs to feel like they are part of the organization. You want to bring someone on board that has an owner vs an employee mentality. What I mean by that is your new team member should feel like the contribution they are making is improving their own financial situation. An employee mentality is quite simply, someone that comes to work every day, just looking for a paycheck. They aren't interested in going above and beyond, because they either don't see the light at the end of the tunnel or they are too lazy to put in the extra effort. Someone with an "owner" mentality will approach their job very differently. I remember going into long conference meetings when I worked as an engineer, and we would discuss all the amazing things we were going to accomplish. When the meeting concluded, no one would take action. Then at the next meeting we would discuss it all over again. This would drive me crazy, I couldn't understand why the managers wouldn't take actions. I eventually became that person that would follow up after the meetings to make sure these items got addressed. This is partially how I knew I was meant to be a business owner. I didn't want to simply come to work every day, do my job and go home. My work was important to me, and when the company succeeded, I felt like I succeeded as well. This is the sort of mentality that I like to look for in future hires.

Surround yourself with team members who are always hungry. I know that may sound strange, but it is imperative that you surround yourself with team members who are always wanting more. While you want people on your team that are hungry, they can't be starving. What I mean by that is that you want individuals who are motivated to put in the time and reap the rewards of their hard work, but not so desperate to get paid that they lose focus or cut corners.

Be as humble as possible and keep in mind that your company's success will not be earned solely by your own merit. Regardless of your title, you should never be too proud to pick up a broom. It keeps you grounded and reminds you that every single person is essential to the success of your company.

Chapter 5 Starting A Business? Money Not Required

There has never been a better time in history to start a business because of all the tools we have available today. A decade ago, starting an e-commerce website required a significant amount of capital and sourcing physical products to sell was very difficult. Nowadays, tools like Shopify & Alibaba make it possible to start an online business and begin generating revenue within a few hours. Shopify acquired Oberlo, which has made it possible to drop ship products on their platform. Therefore you don't even need to necessarily hold inventory. The lack of overhead means you can start a business for very little to no money at all. You will, however, need to drive people to that site (which can be expensive). We will discuss later in this book, how to drive traffic to your site without spending large amounts of money on marketing.

If you're looking for a simple business model, you may want to consider re-selling a product or service that has been undervalued. For example, there are numerous freelance jobs advertised on websites like Fiverr or UpWork that are wildly undervalued. You may notice that a service provider is offering blackboard animations for $5. After you've determined that the provider can deliver on what they are promising, you can advertise the same service for $100 - $500 and outsource the work to this trusted provider. As long as your cost of acquisition (the cost to acquire the customer) is less than what you charge, plus the $5 or so that you pay the service provider, you can make a considerable profit. I know people that have made millions of dollars by identifying poorly marketed products or services and simply marking them up.

There are so many ways to make money nowadays if you just keep your eyes and your mind open. For example. Sophia Amorouso was the creator of the brand "Nasty Gal." According to the Netflix original movie titled "Girl Boss," she got her start by purchasing clothes from thrift stores and selling them on eBay. People buy with their eyes. I have literally purchased used items from yard sales, cleaned them up, taken amazing photos and resold them for 10x or more on marketplaces like eBay. Great photos, great copy, and potentially a great video makes all the difference.

Timing is also important. For example, most big box stores have a large clearance event after a major holiday has passed. Oftentimes the discounts will be as high as 90% off, only a few weeks after the holiday has ended. Imagine purchasing Halloween costumes for 90% off from a major retailer. You can store these costumes in a bin until the beginning of the Halloween season on the following year. Your margins will be very high, so you can list these brand new items for a considerable amount less than the big box shops.

This can make for a considerable profit. If you decide to employ this business model (which is essentially purchasing overstock), I would suggest purchasing evergreen products like a superhero costume that is timeless vs a costume that may not be popular the following year.

You may have heard the old saying that the riches are in the niches. Well, my friend Zach Zelner is a master at monetizing the niches in an efficient and highly profitable manner. Zach was able to build a sales funnel that utilized Facebook marketing to sell over $8M worth of product in only 30 short days. So what did Zach's company sell? A cure for cancer? The hottest new electronic device? Nope, he sold socks. Zach's company, Pup Socks offers pet lovers the ability to purchase customized socks that have a fashionable photo of their pet on them. So as you can imagine, sometimes something as simple as a pair of socks can be highly profitable if marketed to the proper audience.

Chapter 6 Product Market Fit

Let's assume that you've completed the MVP and are now ready to start selling your product or service. How do you get the word out? Well, if you've ever watched the 1989 hit film, "Field Of Dreams," you may remember Kevin Costner's character hearing an ominous voice from the cornfield that said: "If you build it, they will come." Well, unfortunately, this can not be further from the truth when it comes to your business. Even if you've created something that can literally change the world, like a cure for cancer or a fusion energy source, customers will not just magically stumble onto your website. You have to put in the work to build a sales funnel and begin attracting customers to that funnel.

Before going too far down the rabbit hole and spending the company's entire savings on Facebook Ads, you need to understand who your target customer is and how much are they willing to pay for your product or service. If you have a physical product, you may want to consider launching it on a marketplace like Amazon, Walmart.com, eBay, or Etsy. These marketplaces get massive amounts of visitors every day, and it's a great way to identify your target audience, without spending a ton on advertising. The truth is that even if you don't spend a single dollar on advertising, these marketplaces have such a heavy concentration of traffic, it is actually quite possible that customers will eventually find your product and give it a try. I launched one of my first physical product companies on Etsy and sold over $6M on that marketplace alone.

Don't be afraid to ask complete strangers what they think of your business idea. You can do this online via a survey or even hit the streets and ask them face to face. When testing the market, it is never a good idea to ask your friends or family for feedback. Tip of the day... your mom will always love your business idea, regardless of how terrible it is. The ultimate market validation is testing to see if someone will actually pay for it. You may consider setting up a paywall and verifying that people are willing to pay for the product by accepting pre-orders. This method can provide you with the necessary capital to bring the product to market. Whether it's a MOQ (minimum order quantity) for a physical product, additional software work, or other expenses, this method can provide you with working capital while validating the business model. This is a risky method, and you should consult with your legal and/or professional counsel before considering this option.

If you don't have a product that would fair well on a marketplace, there are still several ways that you can promote your product for free. Another way to acquire customers in a very efficient (and oftentimes free) manner is by utilizing social media. If you are selling a product to business professionals (for example), you may want to consider using LinkedIn. Search for professionals that meet your criteria and simply ask them to connect with you. You want to refrain from including the pitch in the invitation to connect. Once you're connected and have built some rapport with a few correspondents under your belt, you can move forward with the pitch.

In a similar fashion, building a significant following on Instagram, Facebook & Twitter can provide you with a sounding board to communicate with your potential customers. Customers buy with their eyes, and in many cases, Instagram is one of the most impactful ways to reach your target audience. Make sure your products look incredible, pay attention to the lighting, and use filters if necessary to get the best results. If you don't have a huge following on social media, you don't necessarily need to spend a ton of money to build that following. We will discuss ways to capitalize on influencer marketing in a later chapter.

Sometimes your target customer is someone very different than the person you had imagined. For example, my friend Adam Mendler owns a company called custom tobacco, that sells custom branded cigar products. He assumed that his target audience consisted entirely of males, but in actuality, he quickly learned that this is not a product men buy for themselves. It was their wives and girlfriends that were purchasing them as gifts and sometimes party planners for a big event. By testing and more importantly, listening to the market, he was able to direct his marketing efforts at the proper audience and his company was a huge success.

Do you remember the story about my friend Zach? He sold $8M worth of socks in such a short period of time because he understood who his target audience was. He created an effective

Facebook marketing strategy and targeted his ads to his narrow customer base efficiently. This is why understanding product market fit is such an important step in building your business. If he didn't do the research, he wouldn't have seen such amazing results.

Chapter 7 The Power Of PR

(my secret weapon)

The internet is full of scammers and consumers are becoming more and more cautious about buying online. When your company is still young and widely unknown, it can be expensive and extremely time-consuming to create the necessary buzz to validate your organization. Over the years, I have perfected several techniques that can help you build your online presence and bring thousands of eyeballs to your website, without spending a dime. I will now share with you, how you can use my secret weapon of PR to validate yourself and your organization.

Public relations is one of the most powerful ways to not only validate the business but to grow your personal brand as well. Utilizing earned media, like a feature in an online publication, a podcast, the radio or television can be a great way to promote your brand. I know what you're thinking, it is very difficult to gain coverage in these publications, but the truth is it is easier than you may think. Find a topic that correlates to the current news cycle and pitch it to the producer of the TV show or a contributor to a publication in which you want to gain coverage. They are much more likely to pick up your story if you have a newsworthy event or if you have a unique perspective on a trending topic. While earned media is powerful, I believe that you will get a greater impact as the interviewer vs the interviewee.

One of my favorite techniques is to turn founders into thought leaders in their space by associating them with existing influencers. Let's assume there is an influencer that could make a huge impact on the success of your company. There are a few "backdoor" approaches that you can use to capitalize on that influencers large social media following, without paying for their services. This may sound crazy, but try approaching their publicist or if they are about to attend a conference, find out who is representing them and introduce yourself. Most influencers won't even answer the phone if their significant other calls, but they will almost always answer if their publicist calls. The truth is that publicists are normally compensated via a monthly retainer, and they want to get their clients as much media exposure as possible. This is where you come in because even though the influencers publicist may be getting them interviews on Good Morning America or some other major outlet, they need to be constantly providing interview opportunities for their clients. I recommend creating a blog, a podcast, or even a publication on a platform like medium. When those publicists have exhausted their big-name connections, they'll likely be open to setting up an interview with your personal blog or podcast. You may have to work your way up to the bigger names, but after you have a few interviews under your belt, you can apply to large online media outlets like Forbes.com to become a contributor. This is a difficult process, but writing for a nationally recognized outlet can help you snag even larger influencers.

PR is like a magic skeleton key that can unlock virtually any door, it all comes down to how you frame the question. Why does this work? The answer is because you're flipping the script. Instead of asking them to do you a favor, you're the one offering to give them something (media coverage) for free. So how does interviewing an influencer help your brand? Imagine you just completed an interview with an influencer and you contacted their publicist to let them know that the article is live.

What do you think it the first thing they're going to do is? The influencer is likely going to share your article across all their social channels, which hopefully amounts to millions of followers. That means a ton of eyeballs on your article. If you interviewed them on a blog that is a on your company's corporate website, I'm sure you can imagine the amount of traffic this will drive to your domain. Let's assume that you posted the article as a contributor for a national publication, how does this help you? Well at the bottom of the article is your byline which has all of your information, including hyperlinks to your social channels and your company website. You now have a very powerful backlink to your site, which can have a huge impact on your SEO ranking. If readers really enjoyed the interview, they may also choose to look into the author (you) even deeper. I've been contacted by countless individuals that wanted to work with me because they read an interview that I'd conducted and tracked me down.

This technique not only applies to influencers, it can also open doors to executives or venture capitalists that would otherwise not take your call. A couple of years ago, I was advising a company that was creating a product in the cryptocurrency mining space. This company required a specific component to build their product and unfortunately, the only manufacturer would not return their emails. Crypto was booming at the time. They were receiving numerous inquiries from startups that didn't have the capital or aptitude to utilize the product. Unknown entities were assumed to be unimportant, so getting a response was virtually impossible. I decided to utilize my secret weapon of PR to resolve this issue. I did some research and was able to contact their PR department. I explained that I wanted to interview their CEO for an article that I was writing for a major publication. The publicist was more than happy to set up the interview. Before the interview started, I built some rapport with the CEO asking questions about his personal life and getting to know him. I then explained that I was advising a startup that had the capital and wherewithal to utilize their component, but that we were hitting a brick wall. He explained that too many unviable startups were contacting them, but he would be more than happy to make a personal introduction to the right people in the organization to get things moving. So why do you think he made the introduction? I believe it is because instead of asking him for something, I was giving him something (PR) and he was simply repaying the favor. It is also quite possible that he wanted a favorable interview, but I would have offered that regardless, it was a great interview. I've used this technique with companies that I mentor on numerous occasions to open doors that would otherwise be closed.

How you frame the question makes all the difference. We work with a co-working space that allows us to utilize their facility to host events and doesn't charge us a penny. Why do they offer this? Because of how we framed the question. Instead of asking them if we could rent out their space, we informed them that we would be hosting an event that will bring dozens of entrepreneurs (their target market) into their facility. We explained that these founders are likely looking for a home base for their company and our event would be a great way for them to check out the space. They realized that the cost of acquisition would be virtually nothing because we would be bringing the guests to their facility. It really is a win-win for everyone. In the same regard, you can gain the exposure from working with an influencer without spending any money. Instead of paying the influencer an exorbitant amount of money to send out a tweet about your company, you can frame the question in another way. By offering the influencer the ability to be featured, you are changing the way the question is framed. You can now capitalize on their social media impact without spending your life savings.

Chapter 8 Perseverance

I remember a few years ago wanting to sell my used car. I used Kelly Blue Book to determine the "value" of that car. Society tells us that one of the most heavily weighted factors when determining the valuation of a car is the vehicle's odometer reading. I would imagine that this is because we as a society have agreed that the more miles we put on a car, the more worn out it becomes. I'd like to argue that this is not always the case. Let's assume that every day you get ready for work, jump into the car, fire up the engine, and drive your vehicle to and from work. After a year or so, you probably have put several thousand miles on the car. And what does society tell us? We are told that the more miles the car has, the more worn out it is and therefore the valuation goes down. However, let's assume that instead of driving that car every day, you were to leave it parked outside your house on the side of the road. I have an RV that I use only a few times per year, and I've noticed that leaving it stationary is not always best. What happens to the tires on a car if they are sitting in the same spot for too long? They begin to get dry rot. And what happens to the engine if moisture begins to work its way into the gears? It may eventually seize. And the gas, does it start to break down? Rodents may find their way into the car as well because no one has moved it. So my point is, even though society tells us that less miles means a better car, the truth is, a car was not designed to sit on the side of the road, unused and just looking pretty. It was designed to propel you down the road to your destination. Cars were designed to be in motion, just like we as humans were not designed to sit in a cubicle or worse sit at home and play video games all day. So my point is, you may suffer from a few setbacks as you go down that long and sometimes difficult road of working on your dreams, but it is important to understand that we as humans were designed to persevere.

Right after college, I took a job that was essentially selling coupons door to door. This was probably one of the most unglamorous jobs I've ever had, but it was also one of the most important. I was extremely shy and could barely get through the interview, let alone cold pitch someone on their front porch. People generally don't like for salesmen to knock on their front door, asking them to purchase something that they probably don't want. Most days I would go home feeling beat up and defeated, the job was commission only and I wasn't even making enough to pay for my gas, but my back was against the wall. I had to support myself, I was hungry and wanted so badly to succeed, so every day I would work harder and harder at the pitch. I got used to hearing people tell me no, and occasionally I'd land a sale or two. I quickly realized that after I received a sale, the next one would be even easier and eventually realized that this was because of my attitude. I would knock on the door with restored confidence and a smile on my face and it would resonate with the customers. I could do a better job of building rapport, which would eventually lead to a sale. Eventually (with the help of my manager), I realized that statistically 1 out of every 20 people would purchase, but only if I had a great attitude. I began to tolerate hearing the word no and instead of letting it bring me down, I would say to myself, one no down, only 19 more to go. As an entrepreneur, you are going to hear the word "no" more than any other time in your life. There are days when you will get knocked down, but it's important to get back up, shake it off, and keep persevering.

The truth is that all aspects of our lives are intertwined. For example: If you lose a big client at work, you'll probably go home with a poor attitude. The sour mood that you now have causes you to get into an argument with your significant other. Now your family life begins to erode and you take that stress back to work. Which will impact your work performance, and the cycle continues. I like to call this "The Cycle Of Crap" because if you don't do something to stop this cycle, it will continuously rob you of your dreams.

Controlling your mindset is one of the most important steps in realizing your dreams. If you've ever read "The Secret," which I highly recommend, you may have heard of the "The Law Of Attraction." In essence, this ideology states that if you put something out into the universe (good or bad), it will eventually come to pass. I could not agree with this more and would like to build on that concept by adding a bit of science to back it up. There is an area of our brains that is known as the reticular activating system (RAS). While I'm sure the RAS has a lot of useful functions, I want to focus on one in particular. The RAS is responsible for determining what is important for us to pay attention to. You may have noticed that after you've decided that you want to purchase a particular car, you suddenly see that model everywhere you look. Well, there aren't more of these cars on the road, it's just because the RAS section of your brain has determined that this is something that is important to you. So imagine if you were to meditate, create a vision board and focus on your goals every single day. The RAS portion of your brain will be constantly looking for ways to make these goals into a reality. Just like you suddenly start noticing more of your vehicle type on the road, you will also start noticing potential partners and opportunities that your mind would otherwise filter out. So by meditating on your goals and reminding yourself of their importance every single day, you really can improve the odds of making them into a reality.

Chapter 9 The End

When you come to the realization that progress is more important than performance, you'll have an entirely new outlook on life. I'm a big fan of Pastor Joel Osteen. He preaches that we go through "seasons" in our lives. When you're in the middle of a long and cold winter, it may feel like spring is never gonna come. Even as you progress towards the next season of your life, the people around you may not notice. A few years ago I got a nasty stomach bug that led to the development of an ulcer. Due to this ailment, I was only able to tolerate rice, oatmeal, and other high carbohydrate meals. In addition, if I let my stomach get too empty, it would begin to burn. So for the better part of a year, I gained a large amount of weight due to this unfortunate health issue. After my stomach got back to "normal," I decided that I wanted to improve my health and lose some weight. Two months in, I noticed the scale was beginning to show major improvements. I was so proud of the progress I was making. Unfortunately, I ran into an old acquaintance that hadn't seen me in a few years. They made a comment on how I looked like I had put on a few pounds. At first, I felt defeated and was about to give up. I felt like reaching my weight loss goals was impossible. I would never get back to my target weight. The real progress, however, happened after I came to the realization that when someone sees me, they are only getting a snapshot of where my life is right now. They just see a guy that is overweight, not a guy that is in transition and making huge strides to reach his goals. So my point is, you must realize that whenever bad things happen in your life, they are only temporary. You may still be overweight, or your company may still be struggling to become profitable, but you're well on your way to changing your life. Others may not see this transformation, but all you need to know is this. Whether it's health issues, money issues, relationship issues, or virtually anything, this is just a season in your life and Spring is just around the corner.

One more quick lesson, hopefully, this one is not too dark. I want to talk about another phenomenon. I was listening to Les Brown the other day. He told a story that really resonated with me. Did you know that human beings are the only creatures in the entire world that are known to suffer from heart attacks on the same day of the week? According to Les, most heart attacks or strokes occur on Monday morning between 8 and 9 AM. It doesn't matter what time zone you're in, it is always between 8 and 9 AM. Why? Well, let's dig into the science. So studies show that between 75% - 85% of Americans hate their jobs. I think we can connect the dots here. Les says that the majority of Americans wake up on Monday morning depressed and dreading the work week that they have ahead of them. They don't want to face that terrible boss and sit in that stuffy cubicle all day, and the stress gets the better of them. I LOVE being an entrepreneur. I love making my own schedule and knowing that my income is 100% based on what I put into it. Entrepreneurship does have its fair share of ups and downs, and it's not for everyone. So my parting words for you are to do something with your life that you love. Something that you're passionate about. Something that makes you happy. Something that makes you want to jump out of bed every morning ready to face the day, instead of hitting that snooze button. Don't be caught by dogma, keep pushing yourself every day. Good luck on your journey. I believe in each and every one of you., You are destined for something amazing.

Go to www.geneswank.com to see how your business dreams can become a reality.